HAL•LEONARD

BLUES PLAY-ALONG

Book & CD for B♭, E♭, Bass Clef and C instruments

VOLUME 8

Blues CLASSICS

PLAY 8 SONGS WITH A PROFESSIONAL BAND

HOW TO USE THE CD:

Each song has <u>two</u> tracks:

1) Full Stereo Mix

All recorded instruments are present on this track.

2) Split Track

Piano and **Bass** parts can be removed
by turning down the volume on the LEFT channel.

Guitar, Harmonica and **Horn** parts can be removed
by turning down the volume on the RIGHT channel.

Cover photo © Blend Images / Alamy

ISBN 978-1-4234-8703-6

HAL•LEONARD® CORPORATION

7777 W. BLUEMOUND RD. P.O. BOX 13819 MILWAUKEE, WI 53213

For all works contained herein:
Unauthorized copying, arranging, adapting, recording, Internet posting, public performance,
or other distribution of the printed or recorded music in this publication is an infringement of copyright.
Infringers are liable under the law.

Visit Hal Leonard Online at
www.halleonard.com

Blues CLASSICS

BOOK

CD

Baby, Please Don't Go
Written by Muddy Waters

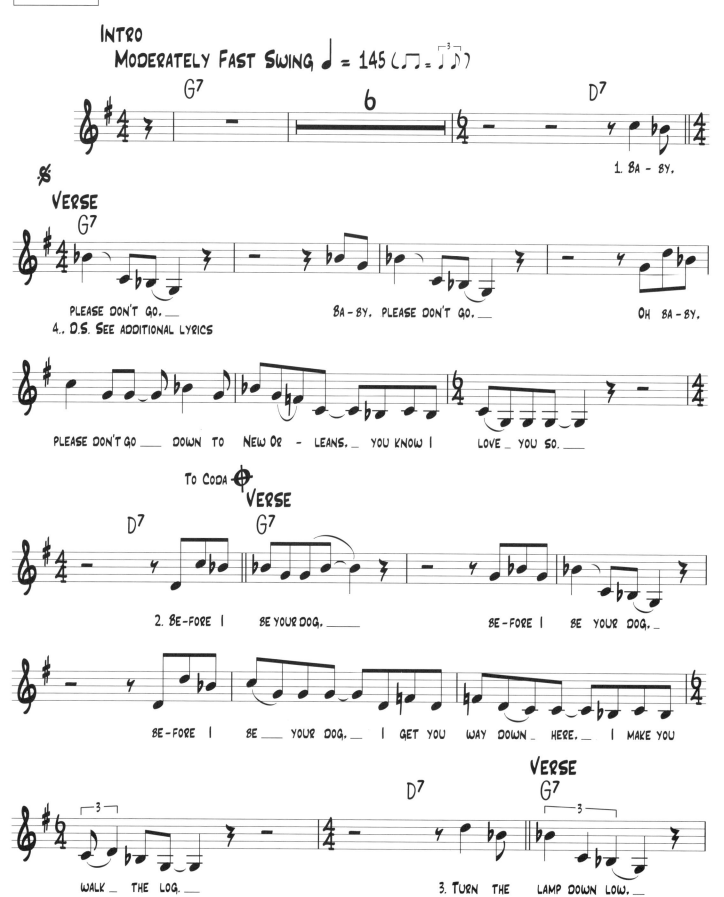

© 1960 (Renewed 1988) Watertoons Music (BMI)/Administered by Bug Music
All Rights Reserved   Used by Permission

TURN THE LAMP DOWN LOW,__ TURN THE LAMP DOWN LOW.__ I BEG YOU

ALL NIGHT LONG.__ BA - BY PLEASE _ DON'T GO.__ COME HERE SON.

GUITAR SOLO

D.S. AL CODA

4. KNOW YOUR

⊕ CODA
GUITAR SOLO

VERSE

5. BA - BY, PLEASE DON'T GO.__ OH BA - BY,

PLEASE DON'T GO,__ OH BA - BY, PLEASE DON'T GO __ DOWN TO

NEW OR - LEANS __ AND GET YOUR COLD ICE __ CREAM. __

ADDITIONAL LYRICS

4. D.S. KNOW YOUR MAN DONE GONE.
KNOW YOUR MAN DONE GONE.
YOU KNOW YOUR MAN DONE GONE
DOWN TO THE COUNTY FARM,
HE GOT HIS SHACKLES ON.

Boom Boom

Words and Music by John Lee Hooker

CD TRACK

2 Full Stereo Mix

10 Split Mix

C Version

Copyright © 1962, 1965 (Renewed) by Conrad Music
All Rights Administered by BMG Chrysalis
International Copyright Secured   All Rights Reserved

C⁷

UP AND DOWN THE FLOOR ___

WHEN YOU'RE TALK - IN' TO ME. ___

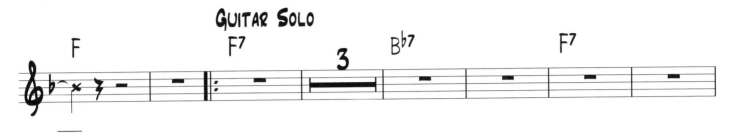

GUITAR SOLO

F   **F⁷**   **3**   **B♭⁷**   **F⁷**

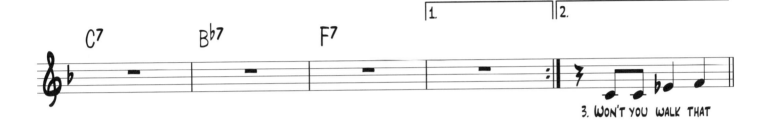

C⁷   **B♭⁷**   **F⁷**

1.   2.

3. WON'T YOU WALK THAT

VERSE

F

WALK   AND   TALK ___ THAT   TALK?

B♭

AND   WHIS - PER   IN   MY   EAR,   TELL   ME   THAT   YOU

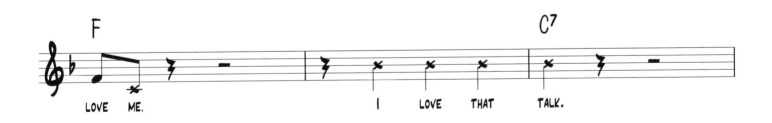

F   **C⁷**

LOVE   ME.   I   LOVE   THAT   TALK,

F

WHEN   YOU   TALK   LIKE   THAT.

7

Born Under a Bad Sign

Words and Music by Booker T. Jones and William Bell

Copyright © 1967 Irving Music, Inc.
Copyright Renewed
All Rights Reserved   Used by Permission

Additional Lyrics

2. I can't read,
   I didn't learn how to write.
   My whole life has been
   One big fight.

3. You know wine and women
   Is all I crave.
   A big leg woman gonna carry me
   To my grave

Dust My Broom

WORDS AND MUSIC BY ELMORE JAMES
AND ROBERT JOHNSON

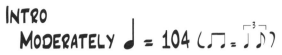

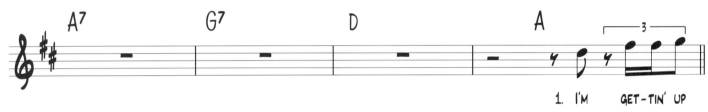

COPYRIGHT © 1951 (RENEWED) BY ARC MUSIC CORP. (BMI)
ALL RIGHTS ADMINISTERED BY BMG CHRYSALIS
INTERNATIONAL COPYRIGHT SECURED ALL RIGHTS RESERVED
USED BY PERMISSION

Additional Lyrics

2. I'm gonna write a letter, telephone every town I know.
   I'm gonna write a letter, telephone every town I know.
   If I don't find her in Mississippi, she's over in Westminster, I know.

3. And I don't want no woman want every downtown man she meets.
   Now, I don't want no woman want every downtown man she meets.
   Means she a no-good, dirty... they shouldn't allow her on the street.

4. I believe, I believe my time ain't long.
   I believe, I believe my time ain't long.
   I'm gonna leave my baby and break up my happy home.

How Long, How Long Blues

Words and Music by Leroy Carr

4. See additional lyrics

Copyright © 1929, 1941 Universal Music Corp.
Copyright Renewed
All Rights Reserved   Used by Permission

ADDITIONAL LYRICS

4. Sometimes I feel so disgusting, and I feel so blue
That I hardly know what in this world, baby, just to do
For how long, how, how, long, baby, how long?

I Ain't Superstitious

Written by Willie Dixon

© 1963 (Renewed 1991) Hoochie Coochie Music (BMI)/Administered by Bug Music
All Rights Reserved   Used by Permission

Additional Lyrics

3. Well, I ain't superstitious, black cat just cross my trail.
   Well, I ain't superstitious, black cat just cross my trail.
   Don't sweep me with no broom, I just might get put in jail.

5. Well, I'm not superstitious, but that black cat out
   'cross my trail.
   Well, I'm not superstitious, a black cat across my trail.
   Don't sweep me with no broom, I just might get put in jail.

It Hurts Me Too

Words and Music by Mel London

Copyright © 1957 (Renewed) Conrad Music (BMI) and Lonmel Publishing (BMI)/Admin. by Bug Music
All Rights for Conrad Music Administered by BMG Chrysalis
All Rights Reserved   Used by Permission

My Babe

Written by Willie Dixon

© 1955 (Renewed 1983) Hoochie Coochie Music (BMI)/Administered by Bug Music
All Rights Reserved   Used by Permission

Bb Version

Baby, Please Don't Go
Written by Muddy Waters

© 1960 (Renewed 1988) Watertoons Music (BMI)/Administered by Bug Music
All Rights Reserved   Used by Permission

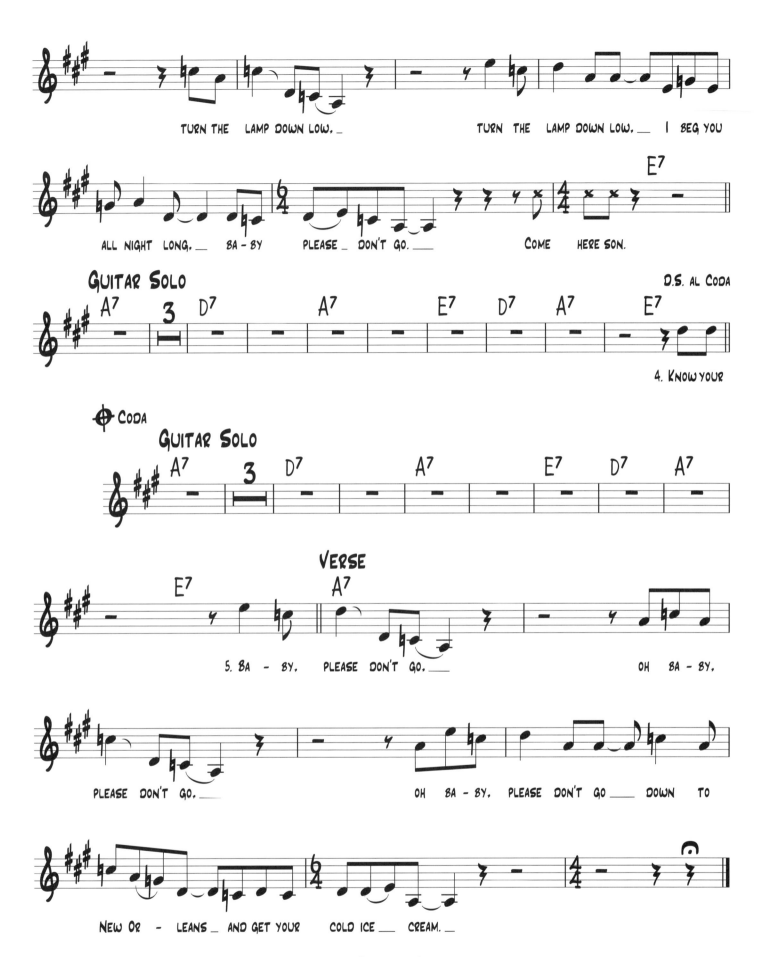

TURN THE LAMP DOWN LOW, ___ TURN THE LAMP DOWN LOW. ___ I BEG YOU

ALL NIGHT LONG. ___ BA - BY PLEASE ___ DON'T GO. ___ COME HERE SON.

Guitar Solo

D.S. AL CODA

4. KNOW YOUR

⊕ Coda

Guitar Solo

Verse

5. BA - BY, PLEASE DON'T GO. ___ OH BA - BY,

PLEASE DON'T GO. ___ OH BA - BY, PLEASE DON'T GO ___ DOWN TO

NEW OR - LEANS ___ AND GET YOUR COLD ICE ___ CREAM. ___

Additional Lyrics

4. D.S. KNOW YOUR MAN DONE GONE,
KNOW YOUR MAN DONE GONE,
YOU KNOW YOUR MAN DONE GONE
DOWN TO THE COUNTY FARM,
HE GOT HIS SHACKLES ON.

Boom Boom

Words and Music by John Lee Hooker

INTRO
MODERATELY FAST SWING ♩ = 158

1. Boom, boom, boom, boom. I'm gon-na shoot you right down.

Right off ___ of your feet. And take you home with me.

Put you in my house. ___ Boom, boom, boom, boom.

2. Ow, how, how, how. Mm. ___

Mm. ___ I love ___ to see you strut.

Copyright © 1962, 1965 (Renewed) by Conrad Music
All Rights Administered by BMG Chrysalis
International Copyright Secured All Rights Reserved

UP AND DOWN THE FLOOR ___ WHEN YOU'RE TALK - IN' TO ME. ___

GUITAR SOLO

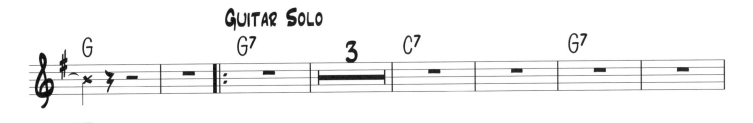

VERSE

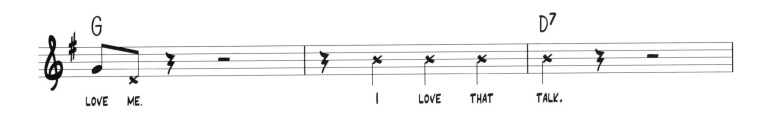

3. WON'T YOU WALK THAT

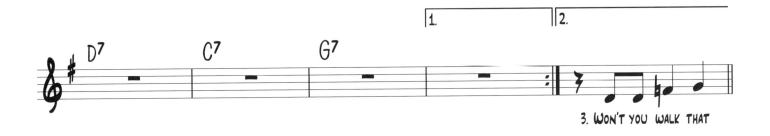

WALK AND TALK ___ THAT TALK?

AND WHIS - PER IN MY EAR. TELL ME THAT YOU

LOVE ME. I LOVE THAT TALK,

WHEN YOU TALK LIKE THAT.

Born Under a Bad Sign

Words and Music by Booker T. Jones and William Bell

Copyright © 1967 Irving Music, Inc.
Copyright Renewed
All Rights Reserved   Used by Permission

To Coda ⊕

GUITAR SOLO

BRIDGE

D.S. al Coda
(Take 3rd ending)

⊕ **CODA**

OUTRO

Repeat and Fade

If it was-n't for bad luck, __ I say, I would-n't have __ no luck __ at all.

Spoken: 'n' that ain't no lie. __

You know if it was-n't for bad __ luck, __

I would-n't have no kind of luck. __ If it was-n't for real __ bad luck, __

I would-n't have __ no luck at all. __

I tell you, I would-n't have __ no luck at all. __ Yeah, __ I'm

A bad luck __ boy! Been hav-in' bad luck all of __

__ my __ days, __ yeah.

Additional Lyrics

2. I can't read,
   I didn't learn how to write.
   My whole life has been
   One big fight.

3. You know wine and women
   Is all I crave.
   A big leg woman gonna carry me
   To my grave

25

Dust My Broom

Words and Music by Elmore James and Robert Johnson

INTRO
Moderately ♩ = 104

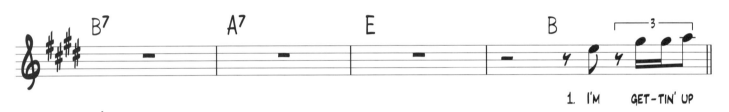

1. I'm get-tin' up

VERSE

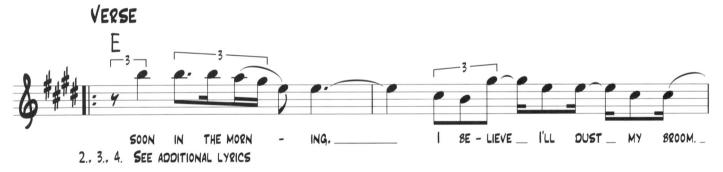

SOON IN THE MORN - ING, _____ I BE-LIEVE __ I'LL DUST __ MY BROOM.

2., 3., 4. See additional lyrics

_____ I'M GET - TIN' UP

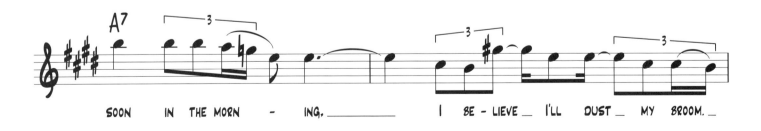

SOON IN THE MORN - ING, _____ I BE-LIEVE __ I'LL DUST __ MY BROOM. __

Copyright © 1951 (Renewed) by Arc Music Corp. (BMI)
All Rights Administered by BMG Chrysalis
International Copyright Secured All Rights Reserved
Used by Permission

Additional Lyrics

2. I'm gonna write a letter, telephone every town I know.
   I'm gonna write a letter, telephone every town I know.
   If I don't find her in Mississippi, she's over in Westminster, I know.

3. And I don't want no woman want every downtown man she meets.
   Now, I don't want no woman want every downtown man she meets.
   Means she a no-good, dirty... they shouldn't allow her on the street.

4. I believe, I believe my time ain't long.
   I believe, I believe my time ain't long.
   I'm gonna leave my baby and break up my happy home.

How Long, How Long Blues

Words and Music by Leroy Carr

Copyright © 1929, 1941 Universal Music Corp.
Copyright Renewed
All Rights Reserved   Used by Permission

Additional Lyrics

4. Sometimes I feel so disgusting, and I feel so blue
That I hardly know what in this world, baby, just to do
For how long, how, how, long, baby, how long?

I Ain't Superstitious

Written by Willie Dixon

Intro
Moderate Swing ♩ = 90

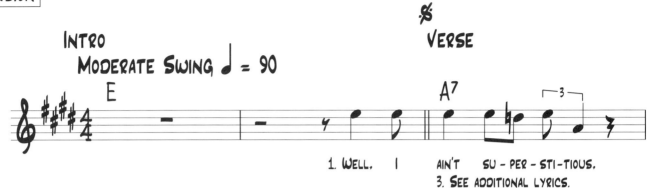

1. Well, I ain't su-per-sti-tious,
3. See additional lyrics.

Black _ cat just cross my trail. ___ Well, I

ain't su-per-sti-tious. But that __ black cat ___ just cross _ my trail.

Don't sweep me with no broom. I might get put in jail. ___

To Coda ⊕
Verse

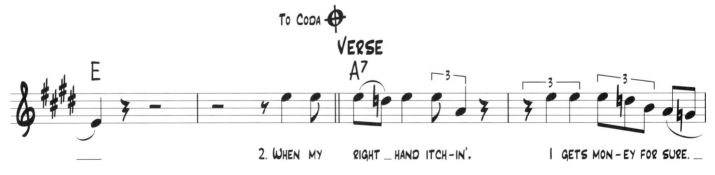

2. When my right _ hand itch-in', I gets mon-ey for sure. _

When my right _ hand itch-in', I gets mon-ey for sure. _

© 1963 (Renewed 1991) Hoochie Coochie Music (BMI)/Administered by Bug Music
All Rights Reserved   Used by Permission

Additional Lyrics

3. Well, I ain't superstitious, black cat just cross my trail.
Well, I ain't superstitious, black cat just cross my trail.
Don't sweep me with no broom, I just might get put in jail.

5. Well, I'm not superstitious, but that black cat out
'cross my trail.
Well, I'm not superstitious, a black cat across my trail.
Don't sweep me with no broom, I just might get put in jail.

It Hurts Me Too

Words and Music by Mel London

Copyright © 1957 (Renewed) Conrad Music (BMI) and Lonmel Publishing (BMI)/Admin. by Bug Music
All Rights for Conrad Music Administered by BMG Chrysalis
All Rights Reserved   Used by Permission

My Babe

Written by Willie Dixon

INTRO

Moderately Fast Swing ♩ = 158

VERSE

1. My ba - by don't stand no cheat - in', _____ my babe.
3. My ba - by don't stand no cheat - in', _____ my ba - by.

Oh _____ yeah, _____ she don't stand no cheat - in', _____
Oh _____ no, _____ she don't stand no cheat - in', _____

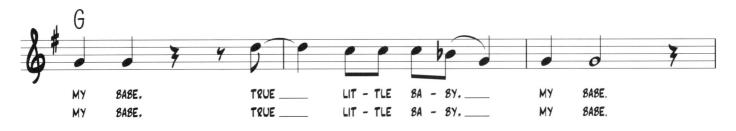

My babe. Oh _____ yeah, _____ she don't
My ba - by. Oh no, _____ she don't

stand no cheat - in'. She don't stand none of that mid - night creep - in'. _____
stand no cheat - in'. Ev - 'ry-thing she do, she do _____ so pleas - in'.

My babe, true _____ lit - tle ba - by, _____ my babe.
My babe, true _____ lit - tle ba - by, _____ my babe.

© 1955 (Renewed 1983) Hoochie Coochie Music (BMI)/Administered by Bug Music
All Rights Reserved Used by Permission

35

Baby, Please Don't Go

Written by Muddy Waters

Eb Version

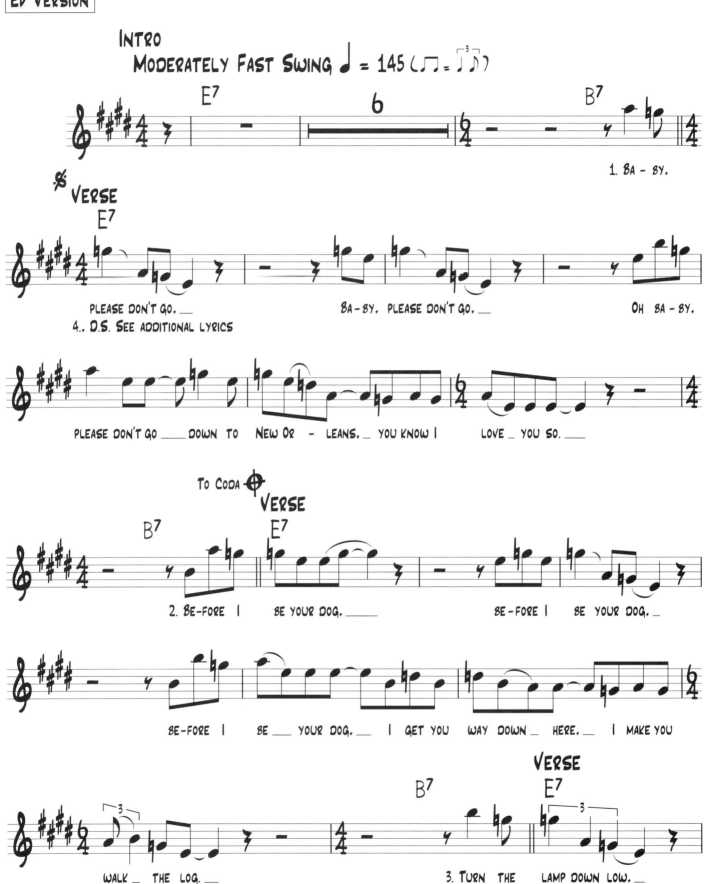

© 1960 (Renewed 1988) Watertoons Music (BMI)/Administered by Bug Music
All Rights Reserved   Used by Permission

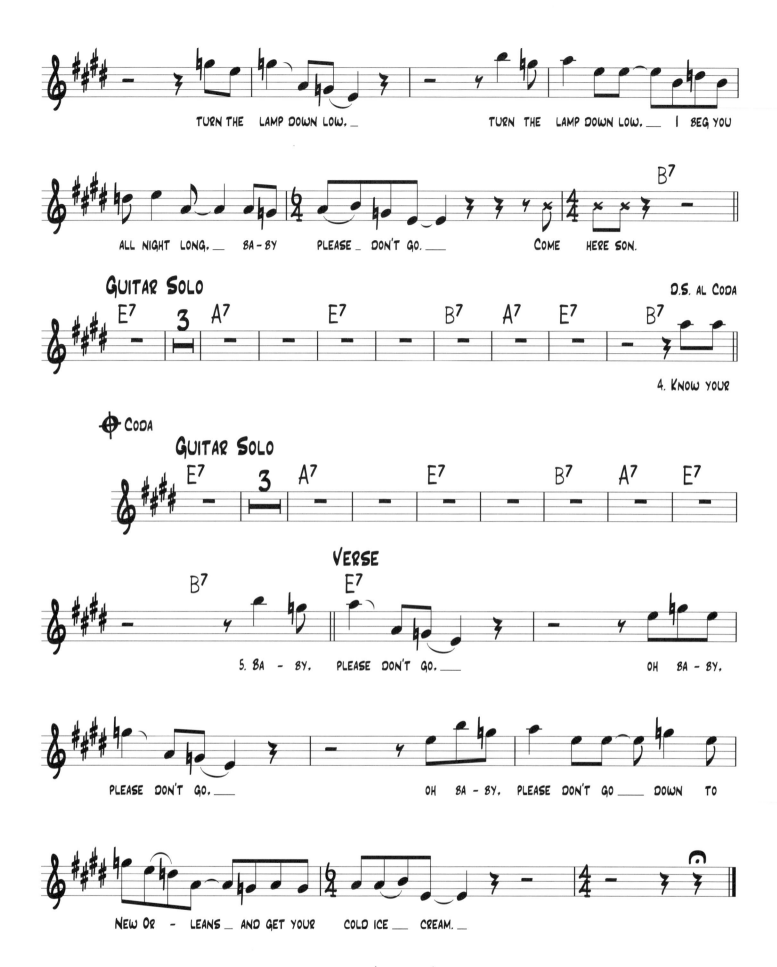

TURN THE LAMP DOWN LOW, ___ TURN THE LAMP DOWN LOW. ___ I BEG YOU

ALL NIGHT LONG, ___ BA - BY PLEASE ___ DON'T GO. ___ COME HERE SON.

GUITAR SOLO

D.S. AL CODA

4. KNOW YOUR

CODA

GUITAR SOLO

VERSE

5. BA - BY, PLEASE DON'T GO, ___ OH BA - BY,

PLEASE DON'T GO, ___ OH BA - BY, PLEASE DON'T GO ___ DOWN TO

NEW OR - LEANS ___ AND GET YOUR COLD ICE ___ CREAM. ___

ADDITIONAL LYRICS

4. D.S. KNOW YOUR MAN DONE GONE,
KNOW YOUR MAN DONE GONE,
YOU KNOW YOUR MAN DONE GONE
DOWN TO THE COUNTY FARM,
HE GOT HIS SHACKLES ON.

CD TRACK

2 Full Stereo Mix
10 Split Mix

Eb Version

Boom Boom

Words and Music by John Lee Hooker

INTRO
MODERATELY FAST SWING ♩ = 158

VERSE

1. Boom, boom, boom. Boom. I'm gon-na shoot you right down. ___

Right off ___ of your feet, and take you home with me.

Put you in my house, ___ Boom, boom, boom. Boom.

VERSE

2. Ow. How. How. How. Mm, _____

Mm, _____ I love ___ to see you strut.

Copyright © 1962, 1965 (Renewed) by Conrad Music
All Rights Administered by BMG Chrysalis
International Copyright Secured   All Rights Reserved

A7

UP AND DOWN THE FLOOR ___   WHEN YOU'RE TALK - IN' TO ME. ___

GUITAR SOLO

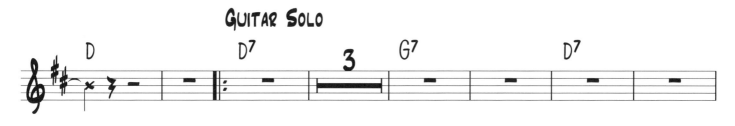

D   D7   **3**   G7   D7

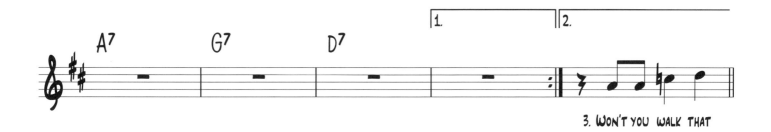

A7   G7   D7   1.   2.

3. WON'T YOU WALK THAT

VERSE

D

WALK   AND   TALK ___ THAT   TALK?

G

AND   WHIS - PER IN   MY   EAR,   TELL   ME   THAT YOU

D   A7

LOVE   ME.   I   LOVE   THAT   TALK,

D

WHEN YOU TALK   LIKE   THAT.

Born Under a Bad Sign

Words and Music by Booker T. Jones
and William Bell

Copyright © 1967 Irving Music, Inc.
Copyright Renewed
All Rights Reserved   Used by Permission

Additional Lyrics

2. I can't read,
I didn't learn how to write.
My whole life has been
One big fight.

3. You know wine and women
Is all I crave.
A big leg woman gonna carry me
To my grave

41

Dust My Broom

Words and Music by Elmore James and Robert Johnson

INTRO
MODERATELY ♩ = 104

VERSE

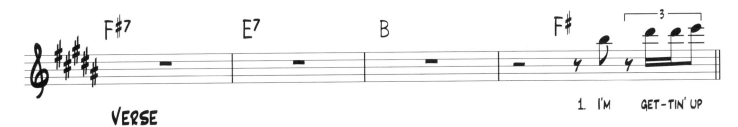

SOON IN THE MORN - ING, _____ I BE - LIEVE _ I'LL DUST _ MY BROOM. _

2., 3., 4. See additional lyrics

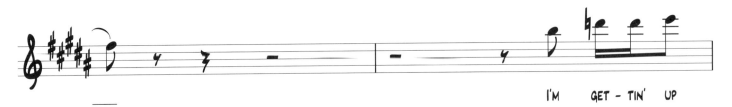

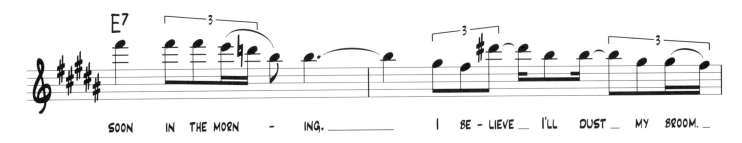

SOON IN THE MORN - ING, _____ I BE - LIEVE _ I'LL DUST _ MY BROOM. _

Copyright © 1951 (Renewed) by Arc Music Corp. (BMI)
All Rights Administered by BMG Chrysalis
International Copyright Secured All Rights Reserved
Used by Permission

ADDITIONAL LYRICS

2. I'M GONNA WRITE A LETTER, TELEPHONE EVERY TOWN I KNOW.
   I'M GONNA WRITE A LETTER, TELEPHONE EVERY TOWN I KNOW.
   IF I DON'T FIND HER IN MISSISSIPPI, SHE'S OVER IN WESTMINSTER, I KNOW.

3. AND I DON'T WANT NO WOMAN WANT EVERY DOWNTOWN MAN SHE MEETS.
   NOW, I DON'T WANT NO WOMAN WANT EVERY DOWNTOWN MAN SHE MEETS.
   MEANS SHE A NO-GOOD, DIRTY... THEY SHOULDN'T ALLOW HER ON THE STREET.

4. I BELIEVE, I BELIEVE MY TIME AIN'T LONG.
   I BELIEVE, I BELIEVE MY TIME AIN'T LONG.
   I'M GONNA LEAVE MY BABY AND BREAK UP MY HAPPY HOME.

How Long, How Long Blues

Words and Music by Leroy Carr

Eb Version

INTRO
MODERATELY SLOW ♩ = 85

1. How long, __

__ BABE, __ HOW LONG __ HAS __ THAT EVE - NIN' TRAIN __ BEEN GONE? __

4. SEE ADDITIONAL LYRICS

To CODA ⊕

__ HOW __ LONG, __ HOW, HOW LONG, BA-BY HOW LONG?

VERSE

2. I __ ASKED HER AT THE STA-TION, "WHY'S MY BA-BY

LEAV-IN' TOWN?" __ YOU WERE DIS - GUST-ED, __ NO-WHERE COULD PEACE BE FOUND. __

FOR HOW __ LONG, __ HOW, HOW LONG, BA-BY HOW

COPYRIGHT © 1929, 1941 UNIVERSAL MUSIC CORP.
COPYRIGHT RENEWED
ALL RIGHTS RESERVED USED BY PERMISSION

I Ain't Superstitious

Written by Willie Dixon

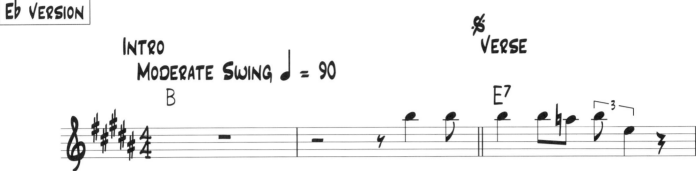

© 1963 (Renewed 1991) Hoochie Coochie Music (BMI)/Administered by Bug Music
All Rights Reserved   Used by Permission

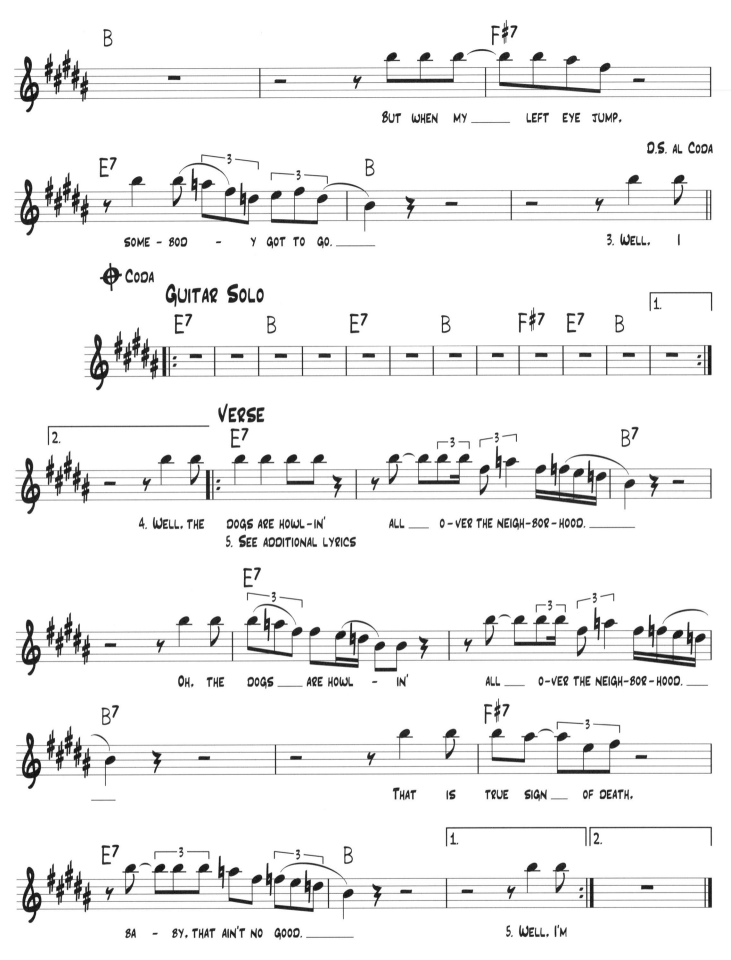

Additional Lyrics

3. Well, I ain't superstitious, black cat just cross my trail.
Well, I ain't superstitious, black cat just cross my trail.
Don't sweep me with no broom, I just might get put in jail.

5. Well, I'm not superstitious, but that black cat out
'cross my trail.
Well, I'm not superstitious, a black cat across my trail.
Don't sweep me with no broom, I just might get put in jail.

It Hurts Me Too

Words and Music by Mel London

Copyright © 1957 (Renewed) Conrad Music (BMI) and Lonmel Publishing (BMI)/Admin. by Bug Music
All Rights for Conrad Music Administered by BMG Chrysalis
All Rights Reserved   Used by Permission

My Babe

Written by Willie Dixon

Intro
Moderately Fast Swing ♩ = 158

Verse

1. My ba - by don't stand no cheat - in', ____ my babe.
3. My ba - by don't stand no cheat - in', ____ my ba - by.

Oh ____ yeah, ____ she don't stand no cheat - in', ____
Oh ____ no, ____ she don't stand no cheat - in', ____

My babe. Oh ____ yeah, ____ she don't
My ba - by. Oh no, ____ she don't

stand no cheat - in', she don't stand none of that mid - night creep - in', ____
stand no cheat - in'. Ev - 'ry-thing she do, she do ____ so pleas - in', ____

My babe. True ____ lit - tle ba - by, ____ my babe.
My babe. True ____ lit - tle ba - by, ____ my babe.

© 1955 (Renewed 1983) Hoochie Coochie Music (BMI)/Administered by Bug Music
All Rights Reserved   Used by Permission

CD TRACK

① Full Stereo Mix

⑨ Split Mix

𝄢 C Version

Baby, Please Don't Go

Written by Muddy Waters

© 1960 (Renewed 1988) Watertoons Music (BMI)/Administered by Bug Music
All Rights Reserved   Used By Permission

TURN THE LAMP DOWN LOW. ___ TURN THE LAMP DOWN LOW. ___ I BEG YOU

D7

ALL NIGHT LONG. ___ BA - BY PLEASE ___ DON'T GO. ___ COME HERE SON.

GUITAR SOLO

D.S. AL CODA

G7   3   C7   G7   D7   C7   G7   D7

4. KNOW YOUR

CODA
GUITAR SOLO

G7   3   C7   G7   D7   C7   G7

VERSE

D7   G7

5. BA - BY, PLEASE DON'T GO. ___   OH BA - BY,

PLEASE DON'T GO. ___   OH BA - BY, PLEASE DON'T GO ___ DOWN TO

NEW OR - LEANS ___ AND GET YOUR COLD ICE ___ CREAM. ___

ADDITIONAL LYRICS

4. D.S. KNOW YOUR MAN DONE GONE,
KNOW YOUR MAN DONE GONE,
YOU KNOW YOUR MAN DONE GONE
DOWN TO THE COUNTY FARM,
HE GOT HIS SHACKLES ON.

BOOM BOOM
WORDS AND MUSIC BY JOHN LEE HOOKER

COPYRIGHT © 1962, 1965 (RENEWED) BY CONRAD MUSIC
ALL RIGHTS ADMINISTERED BY BMG CHRYSALIS
INTERNATIONAL COPYRIGHT SECURED   ALL RIGHTS RESERVED

UP AND DOWN THE FLOOR ___ WHEN YOU'RE TALK - IN' TO ME. ___

GUITAR SOLO

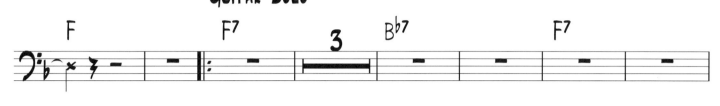

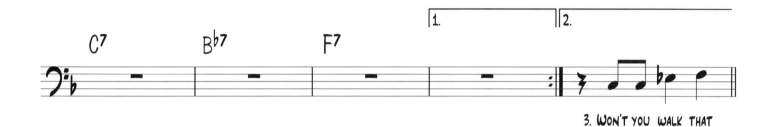

3. WON'T YOU WALK THAT

VERSE

WALK AND TALK ___ THAT TALK?

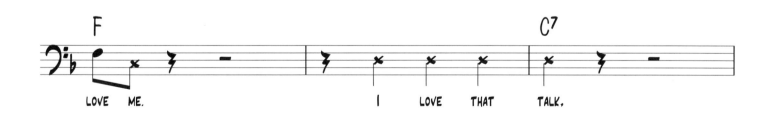

AND WHIS - PER IN MY EAR, TELL ME THAT YOU

LOVE ME. I LOVE THAT TALK.

WHEN YOU TALK LIKE THAT.

Born Under a Bad Sign

Words and Music by Booker T. Jones and William Bell

Copyright © 1967 Irving Music, Inc.
Copyright Renewed
All Rights Reserved   Used by Permission

Additional Lyrics

2. I can't read,
   I didn't learn how to write.
   My whole life has been
   One big fight.

3. You know wine and women
   Is all I crave.
   A big leg woman gonna carry me
   To my grave

Dust My Broom

Words and Music by Elmore James and Robert Johnson

INTRO
MODERATELY ♩ = 104

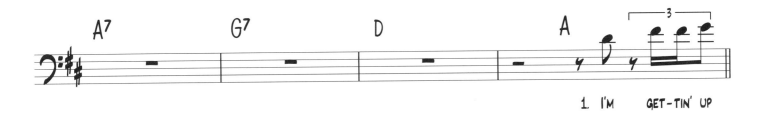

1. I'm get-tin' up

VERSE

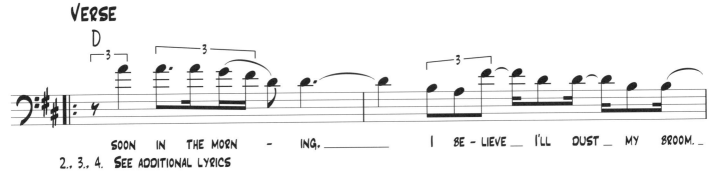

SOON IN THE MORN - ING, _____ I BE-LIEVE _ I'LL DUST _ MY BROOM. _

2., 3., 4. See additional lyrics

I'M GET-TIN' UP

SOON IN THE MORN - ING, _____ I BE-LIEVE _ I'LL DUST _ MY BROOM. _

Copyright © 1951 (Renewed) by Arc Music Corp. (BMI)
All Rights Administered by BMG Chrysalis
International Copyright Secured All Rights Reserved
Used by Permission

Outro-Guitar Solo

Additional Lyrics

2. I'm gonna write a letter, telephone every town I know.
I'm gonna write a letter, telephone every town I know.
If I don't find her in Mississippi, she's over in Westminster, I know.

3. And I don't want no woman want every downtown man she meets.
Now, I don't want no woman want every downtown man she meets.
Means she a no-good, dirty... they shouldn't allow her on the street.

4. I believe, I believe my time ain't long.
I believe, I believe my time ain't long.
I'm gonna leave my baby and break up my happy home.

How Long, How Long Blues

Words and Music by Leroy Carr

Copyright © 1929, 1941 Universal Music Corp.
Copyright Renewed
All Rights Reserved   Used by Permission

I Ain't Superstitious

Written by Willie Dixon

© 1963 (Renewed 1991) Hoochie Coochie Music (BMI)/Administered by Bug Music

All Rights Reserved   Used by Permission

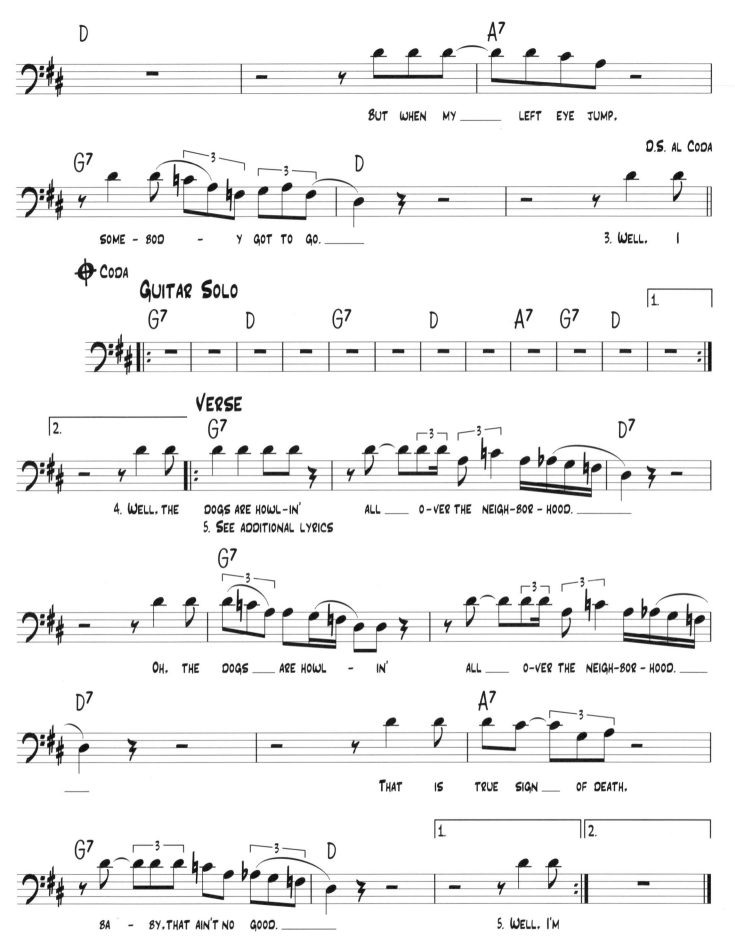

Additional Lyrics

3. WELL, I AIN'T SUPERSTITIOUS, BLACK CAT JUST CROSS MY TRAIL.
   WELL, I AIN'T SUPERSTITIOUS, BLACK CAT JUST CROSS MY TRAIL.
   DON'T SWEEP ME WITH NO BROOM, I JUST MIGHT GET PUT IN JAIL.

5. WELL, I'M NOT SUPERSTITIOUS, BUT THAT BLACK CAT OUT
   'CROSS MY TRAIL.
   WELL, I'M NOT SUPERSTITIOUS, A BLACK CAT ACROSS MY TRAIL.
   DON'T SWEEP ME WITH NO BROOM, I JUST MIGHT GET PUT IN JAIL.

It Hurts Me Too
Words and Music by Mel London

Copyright © 1957 (Renewed) Conrad Music (BMI) and Lonmel Publishing (BMI)/Admin. by Bug Music
All Rights for Conrad Music Administered by BMG Chrysalis
All Rights Reserved   Used by Permission

YOU __ LOVE __ HIM, _____ AND YOU STICK TO HIM LIKE _

__ GLUE. _ BUT THINGS GO WRONG. _____ GO __ WRONG WITH YOU,

IT HURTS __ ME _____ TOO. __

GUITAR SOLO

3. BET-TER QUIT

VERSE

HIM, UH, HE BET-TER PUT YOU DOWN. _ OH, OR I WON'T __

__ STAND _____ TO SEE YOU PUSHED A-ROUND,

'CAUSE WHEN THINGS GO WRONG _____ WITH YOU, _____

IT HURTS __ ME _____ TOO. __

CD TRACK

8 Full Stereo Mix

16 Split Mix

𝄢 C Version

My Babe
Written by Willie Dixon

Intro
Moderately Fast Swing ♩ = 158

1. My ba — by don't stand no cheat - in', ___ my babe.
3. My ba — by don't stand no cheat - in', ___ my ba - by.

Oh ___ yeah, ___ she don't stand no cheat - in', ___
Oh ___ no, ___ she don't stand no cheat - in', ___

My babe.   Oh ___ yeah, ___ she don't
My ba - by.   Oh ___ no, ___ she don't

Stand no cheat - in', she don't stand none of that mid - night creep - in'. ___
Stand no cheat - in'. Ev - 'ry-thing she do, she do ___ so pleas - in'. ___

My babe.   True ___ lit - tle ba - by, ___ my babe.
My babe.   True ___ lit - tle ba - by, ___ my babe.

© 1955 (Renewed 1983) Hoochie Coochie Music (BMI)/Administered by Bug Music
All Rights Reserved Used by Permission

VERSE

F

2. My BA - BY, I KNOW____ SHE LOVE ME,____
4. My BA - BY DON'T STAND NO FOOL - IN',____

MY BABE.
MY BA - BY.

Oh YES,____ I KNOW __
Oh YES,____ SHE DON'T

C

____ SHE LOVE ME, MY BA - BY.
STAND NO FOOL - IN', ____ MY BA - BY.

F

Oh YES, I KNOW____ SHE LOVE __ ME, SHE DON'T DO NOTH-IN' BUT
Oh YES,____ SHE DON'T STAND NO FOOL - IN', WHEN SHE'S HOT, THERE AIN'T

B♭

F

KISS AND HUG __ ME, MY BABE, TRUE ____ LIT - TLE BA - BY, ____
____ NO COOL - IN', ____ MY BABE, TRUE ____ LIT - TLE BA - BY, ____

To Coda ⊕

HARMONICA SOLO

F7

3

B♭7

MY BABE.
MY BABE.

1.

2.

D.S. AL CODA

F7

Gm

C7

F7

⊕ Coda

OUTRO

REPEAT AND FADE

F

SHE'S __ MY BA - BY, SHE'S __ MY BA - BY.

HAL•LEONARD
BLUES PLAY-ALONG

For use with all the C, B♭, Bass Clef and E♭ Instruments, the Hal Leonard Blues Play-Along Series is the ultimate jamming tool for all blues musicians.

With easy-to-read lead sheets, and other split-track choices on the included CD, these first-of-a-kind packages will bring your local blues jam right into your house! Each song on the CD includes two tracks: a full stereo mix, and a split track mix with removable guitar, bass, piano, and harp parts. The CD is playable on any CD player, and is also enhanced so Mac and PC users can adjust the recording to any tempo without changing the pitch!

1. Chicago Blues
All Your Love (I Miss Loving) • Easy Baby • I Ain't Got You • I'm Your Hoochie Coochie Man • Killing Floor • Mary Had a Little Lamb • Messin' with the Kid • Sweet Home Chicago.
00843106 Book/CD Pack $12.99

2. Texas Blues
Hide Away • If You Love Me Like You Say • Mojo Hand • Okie Dokie Stomp • Pride and Joy • Reconsider Baby • T-Bone Shuffle • The Things That I Used to Do.
00843107 Book/CD Pack $12.99

3. Slow Blues
Don't Throw Your Love on Me So Strong • Five Long Years • I Can't Quit You Baby • I Just Want to Make Love to You • The Sky Is Crying • (They Call It) Stormy Monday (Stormy Monday Blues) • Sweet Little Angel • Texas Flood.
00843108 Book/CD Pack $12.99

4. Shuffle Blues
Beautician Blues • Bright Lights, Big City • Further on up the Road • I'm Tore Down • Juke • Let Me Love You Baby • Look at Little Sister • Rock Me Baby.
00843171 Book/CD Pack $12.99

5. B.B. King
Everyday I Have the Blues • It's My Own Fault Darlin' • Just Like a Woman • Please Accept My Love • Sweet Sixteen • The Thrill Is Gone • Why I Sing the Blues • You Upset Me Baby.
00843172 Book/CD Pack $14.99

6. Jazz Blues
Birk's Works • Blues in the Closet • Cousin Mary • Freddie Freeloader • Now's the Time • Tenor Madness • Things Ain't What They Used to Be • Turnaround.
00843175 Book/CD Pack $12.99

7. Howlin' Wolf
Built for Comfort • Forty-Four • How Many More Years • Killing Floor • Moanin' at Midnight • Shake for Me • Sitting on Top of the World • Smokestack Lightning.
00843176 Book/CD Pack $12.99

8. Blues Classics
Baby, Please Don't Go • Boom Boom • Born Under a Bad Sign • Dust My Broom • How Long, How Long Blues • I Ain't Superstitious • It Hurts Me Too • My Babe.
00843177 Book/CD Pack $12.99

9. Albert Collins
Brick • Collins' Mix • Don't Lose Your Cool • Frost Bite • Frosty • I Ain't Drunk • Master Charge • Trash Talkin'.
00843178 Book/CD Pack $12.99

10. Uptempo Blues
Cross Road Blues (Crossroads) • Give Me Back My Wig • Got My Mo Jo Working • The House Is Rockin' • Paying the Cost to Be the Boss • Rollin' and Tumblin' • Turn on Your Love Light • You Can't Judge a Book by the Cover.
00843179 Book/CD Pack $12.99

11. Christmas Blues
Back Door Santa • Blue Christmas • Dig That Crazy Santa Claus • Merry Christmas, Baby • Please Come Home for Christmas • Santa Baby • Soulful Christmas.
00843203 Book/CD Pack $12.99

12. Jimmy Reed
Ain't That Lovin' You Baby • Baby, What You Want Me to Do • Big Boss Man • Bright Lights, Big City • Going to New York • Honest I Do • You Don't Have to Go • You Got Me Dizzy.
00843204 Book/CD Pack $12.99

FOR MORE INFORMATION, SEE YOUR LOCAL MUSIC DEALER, OR WRITE TO:

HAL•LEONARD® CORPORATION
7777 W. BLUEMOUND RD. P.O. BOX 13819 MILWAUKEE, WI 53213

Prices, content, and availability subject to change without notice.

www.halleonard.com

1111

The Best-Selling Jazz Book of All Time Is Now Legal!

SIXTH EDITION

THE REAL BOOK

The Real Books are the most popular jazz books of all time. Since the 1970s, musicians have trusted these volumes to get them through every gig, night after night. The problem is that the books were illegally produced and distributed, without any regard to copyright law, or royalties paid to the composers who created these musical masterpieces.

Hal Leonard is very proud to present the first legitimate and legal editions of these books ever produced. You won't even notice the difference, other than all the notorious errors being fixed: the covers and typeface look the same, the song lists are nearly identical, and the price for our edition is even cheaper than the originals!

Every conscientious musician will appreciate that these books are now produced accurately and ethically, benefitting the songwriters that we owe for some of the greatest tunes of all time!

VOLUME 1
00240221	C Edition	$32.50
00240224	B♭ Edition	$32.50
00240225	E♭ Edition	$32.50
00240226	Bass Clef Edition	$32.50
00240292	C Edition 6 x 9	$27.95
00451087	C Edition on CD-ROM	$25.00
00240302	A-D Play-Along CDs	$24.99
00240303	E-J Play-Along CDs	$24.95
00240304	L-R Play-Along CDs	$24.95
00240305	S-Z Play-Along CDs	$24.99

VOLUME 2
00240222	C Edition	$29.99
00240227	B♭ Edition	$32.50
00240228	E♭ Edition	$32.50
00240229	Bass Clef Edition	$32.50
00240293	C Edition 6 x 9	$27.95
00240351	A-D Play-Along CDs	$24.99
00240352	E-I Play-Along CDs	$24.99
00240353	J-R Play-Along CDs	$24.99
00240354	S-Z Play-Along CDs	$24.99

VOLUME 3
00240233	C Edition	$32.50
00240284	B♭ Edition	$29.95
00240285	E♭ Edition	$29.95
00240286	Bass Clef Edition	$29.95

VOLUME 4
00240296	C Edition	$29.99

VOLUME 5
00240349	C Edition	$32.50

Also available:
00240264	The Real Blues Book	$34.99
00310910	The Real Bluegrass Book	$29.99
00240137	Miles Davis Real Book	$19.95
00240355	The Real Dixieland Book	$29.99
00240235	The Duke Ellington Real Book	$19.99
00240358	The Charlie Parker Real Book	$19.99
00240331	The Bud Powell Real Book	$19.99
00240313	The Real Rock Book	$29.99
00240359	The Real Tab Book – Vol. 1	$32.50
00240317	The Real Worship Book	$29.99

THE REAL CHRISTMAS BOOK
00240306	C Edition	$25.00
00240345	B♭ Edition	$25.00
00240346	E♭ Edition	$25.00
00240347	Bass Clef Edition	$25.00
00240431	A-G Play-Along CDs	$24.99
00240432	H-M Play-Along CDs	$24.99
00240433	N-Y Play-Along CDs	$24.99

THE REAL VOCAL BOOK
00240230	Volume 1 High Voice	$29.95
00240307	Volume 1 Low Voice	$29.99
00240231	Volume 2 High Voice	$29.95
00240308	Volume 2 Low Voice	$29.95
00240391	Volume 3 High Voice	$29.99
00240392	Volume 3 Low Voice	$29.99

THE REAL BOOK – STAFF PAPER
00240327		$9.95

HOW TO PLAY FROM A REAL BOOK
FOR ALL MUSICIANS
by Robert Rawlins
00312097		$14.99

Complete song lists online at www.halleonard.com

Prices and availability subject to change without notice.

FOR MORE INFORMATION, SEE YOUR LOCAL MUSIC DEALER, OR WRITE TO:

HAL•LEONARD® CORPORATION

7777 W. BLUEMOUND RD. P.O. BOX 13819 MILWAUKEE, WI 53213

1111

Presenting the Hal Leonard JAZZ PLAY-ALONG SERIES

For use with all B-flat, E-flat, Bass Clef and C instruments, the Jazz Play-Along® Series is the ultimate learning tool for all jazz musicians. With musician-friendly lead sheets, melody cues, and other split-track choices on the included CD, these first-of-a-kind packages help you master improvisation while playing some of the greatest tunes of all time. FOR STUDY, each tune includes a split track with: melody cue with proper style and inflection • professional rhythm tracks • choruses for soloing • removable bass part • removable piano part. FOR PERFORMANCE, each tune also has: an additional full stereo accompaniment track (no melody) • additional choruses for soloing.

1. **DUKE ELLINGTON**
   00841644 .... $16.95

1A. **MAIDEN VOYAGE/ALL BLUES**
   00843158 .... $15.99

2. **MILES DAVIS**
   00841645 .... $16.95

3. **THE BLUES**
   00841646 .... $16.99

4. **JAZZ BALLADS**
   00841691 .... $16.99

5. **BEST OF BEBOP**
   00841689 .... $16.95

6. **JAZZ CLASSICS WITH EASY CHANGES**
   00841690 .... $16.99

7. **ESSENTIAL JAZZ STANDARDS**
   00843000 .... $16.99

8. **ANTONIO CARLOS JOBIM AND THE ART OF THE BOSSA NOVA**
   00843001 .... $16.95

9. **DIZZY GILLESPIE**
   00843002 .... $16.99

10. **DISNEY CLASSICS**
   00843003 .... $16.99

11. **RODGERS AND HART FAVORITES**
   00843004 .... $16.99

12. **ESSENTIAL JAZZ CLASSICS**
   00843005 .... $16.99

13. **JOHN COLTRANE**
   00843006 .... $16.95

14. **IRVING BERLIN**
   00843007 .... $15.99

15. **RODGERS & HAMMERSTEIN**
   00843008 .... $15.99

16. **COLE PORTER**
   00843009 .... $15.95

17. **COUNT BASIE**
   00843010 .... $16.95

18. **HAROLD ARLEN**
   00843011 .... $15.95

19. **COOL JAZZ**
   00843012 .... $15.95

20. **CHRISTMAS CAROLS**
   00843080 .... $14.95

21. **RODGERS AND HART CLASSICS**
   00843014 .... $14.95

22. **WAYNE SHORTER**
   00843015 .... $16.95

23. **LATIN JAZZ**
   00843016 .... $16.95

24. **EARLY JAZZ STANDARDS**
   00843017 .... $14.95

25. **CHRISTMAS JAZZ**
   00843018 .... $16.95

26. **CHARLIE PARKER**
   00843019 .... $16.95

27. **GREAT JAZZ STANDARDS**
   00843020 .... $16.99

28. **BIG BAND ERA**
   00843021 .... $15.99

29. **LENNON AND MCCARTNEY**
   00843022 .... $16.95

30. **BLUES' BEST**
   00843023 .... $15.99

31. **JAZZ IN THREE**
   00843024 .... $15.99

32. **BEST OF SWING**
   00843025 .... $15.99

33. **SONNY ROLLINS**
   00843029 .... $15.95

34. **ALL TIME STANDARDS**
   00843030 .... $15.99

35. **BLUESY JAZZ**
   00843031 .... $16.99

36. **HORACE SILVER**
   00843032 .... $16.99

37. **BILL EVANS**
   00843033 .... $16.95

38. **YULETIDE JAZZ**
   00843034 .... $16.95

39. **"ALL THE THINGS YOU ARE" & MORE JEROME KERN SONGS**
   00843035 .... $15.99

40. **BOSSA NOVA**
   00843036 .... $15.99

41. **CLASSIC DUKE ELLINGTON**
   00843037 .... $16.99

42. **GERRY MULLIGAN FAVORITES**
   00843038 .... $16.99

43. **GERRY MULLIGAN CLASSICS**
   00843039 .... $16.95

44. **OLIVER NELSON**
   00843040 .... $16.95

45. **JAZZ AT THE MOVIES**
   00843041 .... $15.99

46. **BROADWAY JAZZ STANDARDS**
   00843042 .... $15.99

47. **CLASSIC JAZZ BALLADS**
   00843043 .... $15.99

48. **BEBOP CLASSICS**
   00843044 .... $16.99

49. **MILES DAVIS STANDARDS**
   00843045 .... $16.95

50. **GREAT JAZZ CLASSICS**
   00843046 .... $15.99

51. **UP-TEMPO JAZZ**
   00843047 .... $15.99

52. **STEVIE WONDER**
   00843048 .... $16.99

53. **RHYTHM CHANGES**
   00843049 .... $15.99

54. **"MOONLIGHT IN VERMONT" AND OTHER GREAT STANDARDS**
   00843050 .... $15.99

55. **BENNY GOLSON**
   00843052 .... $15.95

56. **"GEORGIA ON MY MIND" & OTHER SONGS BY HOAGY CARMICHAEL**
   00843056 .... $15.99

57. **VINCE GUARALDI**
   00843057 .... $16.99

58. **MORE LENNON AND MCCARTNEY**
   00843059 .... $15.99

59. **SOUL JAZZ**
   00843060 .... $15.99

60. **DEXTER GORDON**
   00843061 .... $15.95

61. **MONGO SANTAMARIA**
   00843062 .... $15.95

62. **JAZZ-ROCK FUSION**
   00843063 .... $16.99

63. CLASSICAL JAZZ
00843064 ....$14.95

64. TV TUNES
00843065 ....$14.95

65. SMOOTH JAZZ
00843066 ....$16.99

66. A CHARLIE BROWN CHRISTMAS
00843067 ....$16.99

67. CHICK COREA
00843068 ....$15.95

68. CHARLES MINGUS
00843069 ....$16.95

69. CLASSIC JAZZ
00843071 ....$15.99

70. THE DOORS
00843072 ....$14.95

71. COLE PORTER CLASSICS
00843073 ....$14.95

72. CLASSIC JAZZ BALLADS
00843074 ....$15.99

73. JAZZ/BLUES
00843075 ....$14.95

74. BEST JAZZ CLASSICS
00843076 ....$15.99

75. PAUL DESMOND
00843077 ....$14.95

76. BROADWAY JAZZ BALLADS
00843078 ....$15.99

77. JAZZ ON BROADWAY
00843079 ....$15.99

78. STEELY DAN
00843070 ....$14.99

79. MILES DAVIS CLASSICS
00843081 ....$15.99

80. JIMI HENDRIX
00843083 ....$15.99

81. FRANK SINATRA – CLASSICS
00843084 ....$15.99

82. FRANK SINATRA – STANDARDS
00843085 ....$15.99

83. ANDREW LLOYD WEBBER
00843104 ....$14.95

84. BOSSA NOVA CLASSICS
00843105 ....$14.95

85. MOTOWN HITS
00843109 ....$14.95

86. BENNY GOODMAN
00843110 ....$14.95

87. DIXIELAND
00843111 ....$14.95

88. DUKE ELLINGTON FAVORITES
00843112 ....$14.95

89. IRVING BERLIN FAVORITES
00843113 ....$14.95

90. THELONIOUS MONK CLASSICS
00841262 ....$16.99

91. THELONIOUS MONK FAVORITES
00841263 ....$16.99

92. LEONARD BERNSTEIN
00450134 ....$15.99

93. DISNEY FAVORITES
00843142 ....$14.99

94. RAY
00843143 ....$14.99

95. JAZZ AT THE LOUNGE
00843144 ....V$14.99

96. LATIN JAZZ STANDARDS
00843145 ....$14.99

97. MAYBE I'M AMAZED*
00843148 ....$15.99

98. DAVE FRISHBERG
00843149 ....$15.99

99. SWINGING STANDARDS
00843150 ....$14.99

100. LOUIS ARMSTRONG
00740423 ....$15.99

101. BUD POWELL
00843152 ....$14.99

102. JAZZ POP
00843153 ....$14.99

**103. ON GREEN DOLPHIN STREET
& OTHER JAZZ CLASSICS**
00843154 ....$14.99

104. ELTON JOHN
00843155 ....$14.99

105. SOULFUL JAZZ
00843151 ....$15.99

106. SLO' JAZZ
00843117 ....$14.99

107. MOTOWN CLASSICS
00843116 ....$14.99

108. JAZZ WALTZ
00843159 ....$15.99

109. OSCAR PETERSON
00843160 ....$16.99

110. JUST STANDARDS
00843161 ....$15.99

111. COOL CHRISTMAS
00843162 ....$15.99

112. PAQUITO D'RIVERA – LATIN JAZZ*
48020662 ....$16.99

113. PAQUITO D'RIVERA – BRAZILIAN JAZZ*
48020663 ....$19.99

114. MODERN JAZZ QUARTET FAVORITES
00843163 ....$15.99

115. THE SOUND OF MUSIC
00843164 ....$15.99

116. JACO PASTORIUS
00843165 ....$15.99

117. ANTONIO CARLOS JOBIM – MORE HITS
00843166 ....$15.99

118. BIG JAZZ STANDARDS COLLECTION
00843167 ....$27.50

119. JELLY ROLL MORTON
00843168 ....$15.99

120. J.S. BACH
00843169 ....$15.99

121. DJANGO REINHARDT
00843170 ....$15.99

122. PAUL SIMON
00843182 ....$16.99

123. BACHARACH & DAVID
00843185 ....$15.99

124. JAZZ-ROCK HORN HITS
00843186 ....$15.99

126. COUNT BASIE CLASSICS
00843157 ....$15.99

127. CHUCK MANGIONE
00843188 ....$15.99

132. STAN GETZ ESSENTIALS
00843193 ....$15.99

133. STAN GETZ FAVORITES
00843194 ....$15.99

134. NURSERY RHYMES*
00843196 ....$17.99

135. JEFF BECK
00843197 ....$15.99

136. NAT ADDERLEY
00843198 ....$15.99

137. WES MONTGOMERY
00843199 ....$15.99

138. FREDDIE HUBBARD
00843200 ....$15.99

139. JULIAN "CANNONBALL" ADDERLEY
00843201 ....$15.99

141. BILL EVANS STANDARDS
00843156 ....$15.99

150. JAZZ IMPROV BASICS
00843195 ....$19.99

151. MODERN JAZZ QUARTET CLASSICS
00843209 ....$15.99

157. HYMNS
00843217 ....$15.99

162. BIG CHRISTMAS COLLECTION
00843221 ....$24.99

Prices, contents, and availability subject to change without notice.

FOR MORE INFORMATION,
SEE YOUR LOCAL MUSIC DEALER,
OR WRITE TO:

HAL•LEONARD® CORPORATION
7777 W. BLUEMOUND RD. P.O. BOX 13819
MILWAUKEE, WISCONSIN 53213
For complete songlists and more,
visit Hal Leonard online at
www.halleonard.com

*These CDs do not include split tracks.

Jazz Instruction & Improvisation
Books for All Instruments from Hal Leonard

AN APPROACH TO JAZZ IMPROVISATION
by Dave Pozzi
Musicians Institute Press
Explore the styles of Charlie Parker, Sonny Rollins, Bud Powell and others with this comprehensive guide to jazz improvisation. Covers: scale choices • chord analysis • phrasing • melodies • harmonic progressions • more.
00695135 Book/CD Pack $17.95

BUILDING A JAZZ VOCABULARY
By Mike Steinel
A valuable resource for learning the basics of jazz from Mike Steinel of the University of North Texas. It covers: the basics of jazz • how to build effective solos • a comprehensive practice routine • and a jazz vocabulary of the masters.
00849911 ....$19.95

THE CYCLE OF FIFTHS
by Emile and Laura De Cosmo
This essential instruction book provides more than 450 exercises, including hundreds of melodic and rhythmic ideas. The book is designed to help improvisors master the cycle of fifths, one of the primary progressions in music. Guaranteed to refine technique, enhance improvisational fluency, and improve sight-reading!
00311114 ....$16.99

THE DIATONIC CYCLE
by Emile and Laura De Cosmo
Renowned jazz educators Emile and Laura De Cosmo provide more than 300 exercises to help improvisors tackle one of music's most common progressions: the diatonic cycle. This book is guaranteed to refine technique, enhance improvisational fluency, and improve sight-reading!
00311115 ....$16.95

EAR TRAINING
by Keith Wyatt, Carl Schroeder and Joe Elliott
Musicians Institute Press
Covers: basic pitch matching • singing major and minor scales • identifying intervals • transcribing melodies and rhythm • identifying chords and progressions • seventh chords and the blues • modal interchange, chromaticism, modulation • and more.
00695198 Book/2-CD Pack.......................$24.95

EXERCISES AND ETUDES FOR THE JAZZ INSTRUMENTALIST
by J.J. Johnson
Designed as study material and playable by any instrument, these pieces run the gamut of the jazz experience, featuring common and uncommon time signatures and keys, and styles from ballads to funk. They are progressively graded so that both beginners and professionals will be challenged by the demands of this wonderful music.
00842018 Bass Clef Edition...................$16.95
00842042 Treble Clef Edition $16.95

JAZZOLOGY
THE ENCYCLOPEDIA OF JAZZ THEORY FOR ALL MUSICIANS
by Robert Rawlins and Nor Eddine Bahha
This comprehensive resource covers a variety of jazz topics, for beginners and pros of any instrument. The book serves as an encyclopedia for reference, a thorough methodology for the student, and a workbook for the classroom.
00311167 ....$19.99

JAZZ JAM SESSION
15 TRACKS INCLUDING RHYTHM CHANGES, BLUES, BOSSA, BALLADS & MORE
by Ed Friedland
Bring your local jazz jam session home! These essential jazz rhythm grooves feature a professional rhythm section and are perfect for guitar, harmonica, keyboard, saxophone and trumpet players to hone their soloing skills. The feels, tempos and keys have been varied to broaden your jazz experience. Styles include: ballads, bebop, blues, bossa nova, cool jazz, and more, with improv guidelines for each track.
00311827 Book/CD Pack $19.99

JAZZ THEORY RESOURCES
by Bert Ligon
Houston Publishing, Inc.
This is a jazz theory text in two volumes. **Volume 1 includes:** review of basic theory • rhythm in jazz performance • triadic generalization • diatonic harmonic progressions and analysis • substitutions and turnarounds • and more. **Volume 2 includes:** modes and modal frameworks • quartal harmony • extended tertian structures and triadic superimposition • pentatonic applications • coloring "outside" the lines and beyond • and more.
00030458 Volume 1 ....$39.95
00030459 Volume 2 ....$29.95

Prices, contents & availability subject to change without notice.

JOY OF IMPROV
by Dave Frank and John Amaral
This book/CD course on improvisation for all instruments and all styles will help players develop monster musical skills! **Book One** imparts a solid basis in technique, rhythm, chord theory, ear training and improv concepts. **Book Two** explores more advanced chord voicings, chord arranging techniques and more challenging blues and melodic lines. The CD can be used as a listening and play-along tool.
00220005 Book 1 – Book/CD Pack $27.99
00220006 Book 2 – Book/CD Pack $24.95

THE PATH TO JAZZ IMPROVISATION
by Emile and Laura De Cosmo
This fascinating jazz instruction book offers an innovative, scholarly approach to the art of improvisation. It includes in-depth analysis and lessons about: cycle of fifths • diatonic cycle • overtone series • pentatonic scale • harmonic and melodic minor scale • polytonal order of keys • blues and bebop scales • modes • and more.
00310904 ....$14.95

THE SOURCE
THE DICTIONARY OF CONTEMPORARY AND TRADITIONAL SCALES
by Steve Barta
This book serves as an informative guide for people who are looking for good, solid information regarding scales, chords, and how they work together. It provides right and left hand fingerings for scales, chords, and complete inversions. Includes over 20 different scales, each written in all 12 keys.
00240885 ....$17.99

21 BEBOP EXERCISES
by Steve Rawlins
This book/CD pack is both a warm-up collection and a manual for bebop phrasing. Its tasty and sophisticated exercises will help you develop your proficiency with jazz interpretation. It concentrates on practice in all twelve keys – moving higher by half-step – to help develop dexterity and range. The companion CD includes all of the exercises in 12 keys.
00315341 Book/CD Pack $17.95

FOR MORE INFORMATION, SEE YOUR LOCAL MUSIC DEALER, OR WRITE TO:

HAL•LEONARD® CORPORATION
7777 W. BLUEMOUND RD. P.O. BOX 13819 MILWAUKEE, WI 53213

Visit Hal Leonard online at
www.halleonard.com

0911